BOLIVIA: HUMAN RIGHTS

EXECUTIVE SUMMARY

Bolivia is a constitutional, multi-party republic with an elected president and a bicameral legislature. In December 2009, in a process deemed free and fair by international observers, citizens re-elected as president Evo Morales Ayma, leader of the Movement Toward Socialism Party. Authorities maintained effective control over the security forces, but there were allegations that security forces committed human rights abuses.

The most serious human rights problems included widespread corruption and inefficiency in the country's law enforcement and judicial system, leading to arbitrary arrest or detention and denial of a fair and timely public trial, as well as violence against women.

Additional human rights problems included harsh prison conditions, restrictions on freedom of speech and press, lack of government transparency, trafficking in persons, and vigilante justice. Societal discrimination continued against women; members of racial and ethnic minority groups; indigenous persons; individuals with disabilities; lesbian, gay, bisexual, and transgender (LGBT) persons; and those with HIV/AIDS.

The government took steps in some cases to prosecute security service and other government officials who committed abuses; however, inconsistent application of the laws and a dysfunctional judiciary led to impunity.

Section 1. Respect for the Integrity of the Person, Including Freedom from:

a. Arbitrary or Unlawful Deprivation of Life

There were reports that the government or its agents committed arbitrary or unlawful killings. The legal mechanism to investigate and punish internal abuse and corruption remained suspended and unenforced through the year. Military authorities refused to provide information about at least six deaths of military personnel. For instance, on July 18, Santa Cruz Aviation Academy Cadet Wildo Daniel Delgado was shot and killed, but the military did not provide any information about the incident. On August 1, Defense Minister Ruben Saavedra told a congressional committee that 20 members of the armed forces had been killed as a result of internal accidents and possibly murder since 2010, of which 11 were a result of drowning. He did not release specific information about the cases.

On January 19, the Constitutional Court denied the military's appeal to maintain jurisdiction in the case of Sub-lieutenants Jorge Castro Urena, Rudy Gerardo Flores Herrera, Franz Eduardo Garcia, and Roberto Roya Velasquez, all charged with the 2011 murder of Sub-lieutenant Grover Poma Guanto. The court ruled that civilian courts must adjudicate cases in which the military or its leaders are accused of committing human rights abuses. The military did not comply with the court's ruling and on July 7 prosecutor Gilbert Munoz opened a case against the military for refusing to turn over all of the information related to the Poma case. Munoz' petition was pending at year's end.

b. Disappearance

There were no reports of politically motivated disappearances.

c. Torture and Other Cruel, Inhuman, or Degrading Treatment or Punishment

The constitution and laws prohibit such practices, but there were at least two reports that government officials employed them.

Brazilian citizen Adao Nilson Souza da Silva alleged that police apprehended and tortured him for nearly five hours on April 18 to coerce his confession to a high-profile murder. Souza reported that police suffocated him by forcing his head into a plastic bag. Legal authorities held Souza in preventive detention from April 18 until April 26, when another individual confessed to the murder. The government did not investigate the incident nor file charges against the police for the alleged torture.

On September 12, soldier Freddy Rodriguez alleged that a military instructor and other soldiers assaulted him on a military base in Tupiza, Potosi Department. Rodriquez was treated in the Eduardo Eguia Hospital in Potosi, and the local military authority pledged to investigate the alleged abuse within a 10-day period. Authorities released no information about the internal military investigation by year's end.

Prison and Detention Center Conditions

Prison conditions were harsh due to overcrowding. Authorities acknowledged that due to corruption among low-ranking and poorly paid guards, the state was unable to regulate inmates within facilities. A lack of internal control created an unsafe environment, resulting in at least 36 inmate deaths. Hundreds of children lived in the unsafe penitentiary centers, leading to several cases of child abuse and at least two children's deaths. Many prisoners were forced to pay bribes for protection and accommodation.

Physical Conditions: Prisons and detention centers were overcrowded and underfunded. On September 2, the National Penitentiary System announced there were 14,771 inmates, an increase of 1,282 since the end of 2012, in a system designed for between 5,000 and 5,750. The human rights ombudsman reported that as of July, 13 percent of the prison population was female. During the year 236 inmates received pardons as a result of a December 2012 executive order allowing for the release of up to 1,600 inmates. Severe bureaucratic delays and lack of access to legal counsel limited the number of inmates who received pardons. On September 11, President Morales issued an executive order to pardon up to 2,000 inmates, but by November 1, authorities had released only seven inmates.

Government authorities announced that the penitentiary system's capacity for inmates increased by 750 through the addition of a 450-person rehabilitation center in Yacuiba, Tarija Department, on June 4, and a 300-inmate facility in Patacamaya, La Paz Department, on August 19. The media reported a lack of water and electricity prevented the Yacuiba facility from accommodating the 450 inmates projected and that as of October 29, the Patacamaya facility held 161 inmates.

Due to a lack of internal policing, violence and riots among prisoners remained a problem. On April 11, inmates in Santa Cruz's Palmasola prison killed inmate Carlos Enrique Pereira Marisa, but authorities did not investigate his death. On August 23, a fire started during a violent conflict between two groups of inmates in Palmasola prison killed 35 people, including an 18-month-old child. Government authorities responded by moving 10 inmates suspected of leading the conflict to Chonchocoro prison in La Paz Department.

There are three women's prisons located in La Paz, Cochabamba, and Trinidad. In Morros Blancos Prison in Tarija, Montero Prison in Santa Cruz, Riberalta Prison in Beni, and Oruro Prison in Oruro, men and women shared sleeping facilities. In the other facilities, men and women maintained separate sleeping quarters, but the populations comingled daily. Conditions for female inmates were similar to those for men. Pretrial detainees were held with convicted prisoners. According to government ministry officials, 1,000 convicted juveniles (ages 16 to 21) were not segregated from adult prisoners in jails. Adult inmates and police reportedly abused juvenile prisoners. On January 17, National Penitentiary Director Ramiro Llanos ordered the relocation of 42 juveniles from the Calahuma facility in Viacha, La Paz Department, to San Pedro Prison in La Paz due to allegations of hazing and torture by police guards. After parents of the minors protested the relocation to the overcrowded San Pedro. Authorities returned the juvenile inmates to Calahuma on January 18. Rehabilitation programs for juveniles or other prisoners were scarce.

Although the law permits children up to the age of six to live with an incarcerated parent, children as old as 12 lived with a parent, usually their mothers, in prison. According to the Ministry of Education's Alternative Education Program data released in June, at least 2,100 children and adolescents lived in the country's penitentiaries: 1,197 were younger than age six, while 903 were older than the legal limit of six. The government took some steps to relocate children from the country's prison facilities. On July 10, San Pedro Prison Warden Carlos Coritza announced that officials had removed 40 to 50 minors from the facility; on July 16, Santa Cruz Social Policy Director Duberti Soleto announced that he had evacuated 96 minors; and on July 27, Human Rights Ombudsman Legal Advisor David Lopez announced that authorities had relocated 40 minors from the Morros Blancos Prison in Tarija.

There were reports of abuse of children living in prison facilities. On June 10, authorities at Santa Cruz's Palmasola prison discovered that an inmate had sexually abused a six-year-old boy living in the facility, and on June 20, La Paz's San Pedro Prison authorities found a 12-year-old girl, whose incarcerated father, uncle, and godfather sexually abused her over a five-year period in the prison. Unsafe health conditions put children living in prison facilities at risk. After a meningitis outbreak in La Paz's San Pedro Prison, resulting in the deaths of a woman and child on June 1, National Penitentiary Director Ramiro Llanos ordered evacuation of the estimated 236 minors living in the facility but canceled his directive after authorities were unable to secure temporary shelter for the minors.

Due to persistent corruption, a prisoner's wealth often determined cell size, visiting privileges, ability to attend court hearings, day-pass eligibility, and place and length of confinement. In San Pedro Prison, the main facility in La Paz, officials demanded bribes of 686 to 6,860 bolivianos ($100 to $1,000) from inmates before assigning them to cells, leaving at least 180 inmates to sleep in hallways and open-air spaces. The media reported some rural facilities held as many as 45 inmates in the same cell. Inmates alleged there were an insufficient number of police officers to escort inmates to their judicial hearings, further delaying cases. Inmates also claimed that police demanded bribes in exchange for allowing them to attend hearings.

Services to sustain basic needs were inadequate. Prisoners had access to potable water, but the standard prison diet was insufficient, and prisoners who could afford it supplemented rations by buying food. National Penitentiary Director Ramiro Llanos declared that the state allocated the equivalent of 6.4 bolivianos ($0.92) for a prisoner's daily diet and 3.2 bolivianos ($0.46) for the diet of underage children living with their inmate parents. The law provides that prisoners have access to medical care, but care was inadequate, and it was difficult for prisoners to obtain permission for outside medical treatment. On September 2, inmates in the new Patacamaya prison protested, alleging a lack of food, hot water, and beds in the facility.

Administration: Recordkeeping on prisoners was adequate and maintained by the penitentiary system's national office. Alternatives to sentencing for nonviolent offenders were not used. Authorities provide detainees reasonable access to visitors and permit observance of their religious practices. Authorities permitted prisoners to submit complaints periodically to a commission of district judges for investigation; however, due to fear of retaliation by prison authorities, inmates frequently did not submit complaints of abuses.

Independent Monitoring: The government generally permitted prison visits by independent nongovernmental observers such as International Committee of the Red Cross, judges, and media representatives, and such visits took place during the year.

d. Arbitrary Arrest or Detention

The law prohibits arbitrary arrest and detention, but in some cases security forces seized and held individuals under legally questionable circumstances.

On September 4, law enforcement officials illegally detained Luis Vasquez, lawyer to National Convergence Party Senator Roger Pinto, who was in exile in Brazil, at the Santa Cruz Viru Viru Airport for eight hours. Vasquez was en route to Brazil to advise Pinto about his legal affairs (see section 2.d.).

The case against former Central Bank president (1995-2006) Juan Antonio Morales, charged with illicit enrichment for bonuses he received and granted to bank employees in 1995-97, continued at year's end. Despite the Constitutional Court's October 2012 decision to strike down the anticorruption law's retroactivity clause, under which authorities brought the charges against Morales, the government did not dismiss the case. In addition, the lead prosecutor overseeing the investigation, Harry Suaznabar, was accused of involvement in the extortion network uncovered by the Jacob Ostreicher case, and he fled the country in January (see section 4). Since his arrest in 2011, Morales remained under house arrest, although the government granted him permission to teach at a university.

Role of the Police and Security Apparatus

The national police have primary responsibility for law enforcement and the maintenance of order within the country, but military forces may be called to help in critical situations. The police report to the Ministry of Government, and the military forces report to the Ministry of Defense. The legal mechanism to investigate and punish internal abuse and corruption remained suspended and unenforced through the year as a result of national police strikes in June 2012, when the government agreed to revise the code. On May 22, Vice Minister of Government for Citizen Security Humberto Echalar announced that the government would resume negotiations with the National Police Association about implementing the new disciplinary law, but the parties did not reach agreement by year's end.

Arrest Procedures and Treatment of Detainees

The law requires that police obtain an arrest warrant from a judge and that the police inform the prosecutor of an arrest within eight hours. The law also mandates that a detainee appear before a judge within 24 hours (except under a declared state of siege, in which a detainee may be held for 48 hours), at which time the judge must determine the appropriateness of continued pretrial detention or release on bail. The judge shall order the detainee's release if the prosecutor fails to show sufficient grounds for arrest. The state allows suspects to select their own lawyers, and the state also provides a lawyer from the public defender's office if the suspect requests one.

Arbitrary Arrest: Legal authorities neither presented formal charges nor dismissed the case against U.S. citizen Jacob Ostreicher in violation of the legal limit of 180 days to complete the investigation process and present charges against a suspect.

Ostreicher returned to the United States December 16. Police arrested Ostreicher in 2011 for suspicion of money laundering and affiliation with a criminal organization, placed him in preventive detention, and held him until December 2012, when he was released under house arrest. In November and December 2012, authorities arrested more than a dozen government officials on allegations of extortion related to the case, but none of the officials had been tried by year's end. The government alleged that corrupt officials pressured the judge to reverse his initial decision to grant Ostreicher bail in 2011 and to postpone court hearings in his case more than 20 times. The government also alleged that during Ostreicher's imprisonment, the arrested officials illegally sold Ostreicher's business assets and stole the proceeds (see section 4). On February 20, President Morales called on Ostreicher to prove the origin of his investments in the country, despite the fact that Ostreicher had not been charged with a crime.

Pretrial Detention: A national penitentiary report released in September confirmed that 83 percent of all inmates, 12,260 individuals, were in preventive detention. The law affords judges the authority to order preventive detention if there is a high probability that a suspect committed a crime, if evidence exists that the accused seeks to obstruct the investigation process, or if a suspect is considered a flight risk. If a suspect is not detained, a judge may order significant restrictions on the suspect's movements. Detainees generally had prompt access to their families and access to lawyers. Approximately 70 percent of detainees could not afford legal counsel, and the public defenders assigned to their cases were overburdened.

The Construir Foundation, a human rights nongovernmental organization (NGO), reported in May that prosecutors and judges relied heavily on preventive detention. The report found that prosecutors seek preventive detention for suspects in 70 percent of cases and that judges order preventive detention in 54 percent of cases. In Santa Cruz, which had the country's largest prison population, judges ordered preventive detention of suspects in 86 percent of all cases.

Denial of justice due to prolonged preventive detention remained a problem. Although the law establishes that the investigatory phase and the trial phase of a case shall not exceed 36 months combined, the Construir Foundation estimated approximately 75 percent of suspects remained in preventive detention longer than the legal limits. The law states that no one shall be detained for more than 18 months without formal charges. If after 18 months the prosecutor does not present formal charges and conclude the investigatory phase, the detainee may request release by a judge. The judge must order the detainee's release, but the charges against the detainee are not dropped. Judicial corruption, a shortage of public defenders, inadequate case-tracking mechanisms, and complex criminal justice procedures kept many suspects detained for more than 18 months before trial.

On February 8, Judge Estrella Monano Ocampo ordered the immediate release of Luis Cordoba Marca, who had been held for more than 21 years in preventive detention in Santa Cruz's Palmasola Prison. Cordoba alleged government authorities never informed him about the nature of the charges against him. On July 24, a representative of the Santa Cruz Human Rights Ombudsman's Office announced its concern about the case of Palmasola inmate Zacarias Navia Navia, who had been held in preventive detention for more than 23 years without a sentence. On December 5, the government released Navia.

Children from 11 to 16 years of age may be detained indefinitely in children's centers for known or suspected offenses or for their protection on the orders of a social worker. There is no judicial review of such orders.

e. Denial of Fair Public Trial

The law provides for an independent judiciary, but the judiciary was corrupt and overburdened. In September, Council of Magistrates President Cristina Mamani stated that the backlog of cases was 500,000 and that there were only 815 judges nationwide. A report by the Construir Foundation, the Catholic University in La Paz, and the UN's Office of the High Commissioner for Human Rights stated that in urban jurisdictions only 10 new department prosecutors were hired between 2008 and 2012 and that criminal court judges had a backlog of nearly 129,000 cases. Authorities generally respected court orders but sometimes levied charges against judges to pressure them to change their verdicts.

On August 15, the Ministry of Transparency's Institute of Studies in Transparency and Corruption released a report citing the average judicial delays in corruption cases. The study reported that although the law mandates that the investigation process of a case cannot exceed 180 days, the average length of a corruption case investigation was 417 days. The study also found that instead of the 20-day period required between the formal charge and the first court hearing, the average case took 454 days to come before a judge or jury.

Trial Procedures

The constitution and law provide for the right to be informed of charges promptly and in detail and for a fair trial without undue delay. Defendants enjoy the right to presumption of innocence and trial by jury. They also have the right to consult an attorney, adequate time and facilities to prepare a defense, confront adverse witnesses, present witnesses and evidence, access government-held evidence, and file an appeal. Defendants who cannot afford an attorney have the right to a public defender or private attorney at public expense.

On February 5, former Pando governor Leopoldo Fernandez of the Democratic and Social Power (PODEMOS) Party, on trial for assault and homicide, was released from prison and ordered to serve house arrest due to his poor medical condition. In 2011 his detention period exceeded the three-year limit on detention without a conviction, but his trial continued at year's end. On July 25, Vice Minister of Environment Jorge Barahona announced the government was in the process of expropriating Fernandez's 7,413-acre farm in Pando due to a lack of productivity that harmed the local community's economic interest, a move that Fernandez called "political persecution."

In at least one case, judicial authorities did not accommodate a suspect's health condition, possibly contributing to his death. On October 12, former president of the National Highway Service Jose Maria Bakovic suffered a heart attack and died in La Paz. Bakovic's lawyer Audalia Zurita stated that legal authorities mandated his client's presence at a court hearing in La Paz, despite medical professionals' warnings that he could not travel from his home in Cochabamba to the high altitude region without serious risks to his health.

Political Prisoners and Detainees

While there were no reports of political prisoners or detainees, opposition members alleged that charges against some elected officials were politically motivated (see section 3).

Civil Judicial Procedures and Remedies

There is a judiciary process for civil matters, and the law provides for criminal remedies for human rights violations. At the conclusion of a criminal trial, the complainant can initiate a civil trial to seek damages. The ombudsman for human rights can issue administrative resolutions on specific human rights cases, which the government may enforce (the ombudsman's resolutions are nonbinding. The state does not have to accept his recommendations). Cases involving violations of an individual's human rights may be submitted through petitions by individuals or organizations to the Inter-American Commission of Human Rights (IACHR), which in turn may submit the case to the Inter-American Court of Human Rights. The court can order civil remedies including fair compensation to the individual injured.

f. Arbitrary Interference with Privacy, Family, Home, or Correspondence

The law prohibits such actions, and the government generally respected these prohibitions.

Section 2. Respect for Civil Liberties, Including:

a. Freedom of Speech and Press

The constitution and law provide for freedom of speech and press, but the government did not always respect these rights. The government used the antiracism law to restrict both rights, and some media outlets reported the government pressured them to report favorably about its policies. Some members of the press also alleged that government officials verbally harassed individual journalists and intimidated media outlets perceived to be critical of the government.

Freedom of Speech: The lawsuit brought under the 2010 antiracism law against television presenter Milena Fernandez by Oruro Mayor Rossio Pimental in July 2012 continued unresolved. On January 29, Vice Minister of Decolonization Felix Cardenas announced his office would join the case against Fernandez, who stated during a July 2012 television program that the city of Oruro was "foul smelling." Hearings in the case on both October 13 and November 5 were cancelled, and the case was pending at year's end.

Press Freedoms: Some media outlets alleged the government pressured news organizations to report favorably about government policies and retaliated against news organizations that did not comply. Journalists alleged the government's retaliatory tactics included withdrawing all of its advertisements, thus denying a significant source of revenue, and launching stringent tax audits, forcing companies to spend time and resources to defend themselves.

The Presidency Ministry's August 2012 lawsuit against the Fides News Agency and daily newspapers *Pagina Siete* and *El Diario* under the antiracism law for spreading and inciting racism remained unresolved. The government brought the charges after the newspapers published headlines claiming President Morales called eastern, lowland individuals lazy.

The Bolivian Broadcasting Association continued to express concern about the 2011 telecommunications law that mandates the redistribution of broadcasting licenses and provides the government with a 33 percent share of the licenses. The association asserted the law would restrict freedom of expression and stated it could lose 400 broadcasters to the government when their licenses expire in 2017.

Violence and Harassment: There were reports of violence and harassment against members of the press corps. There were also allegations that government officials targeted and harassed media outlets perceived to be critical of the government. In February, the National Observatory for Media Outlets and the Unite Foundation reported that in 2012 there were at least 81 cases of verbal and physical aggression against 130 media-sector employees. The National Press Association, which represents 20 media outlets, reported there were 33 cases of violent assault and 27 cases of verbal harassment against its journalists in 2012.

On May 21, protesters who accused the station of biased reporting broke into the station of Radio AM 1080 "Voice of the Majority" in Caranavi, La Paz Department. The protesters threatened to kill journalist Franz Eddy Loza and technician Juan Carlos Mazarro, and they destroyed the station's equipment. On May 22, the Ministry of Communication condemned the act as "an attack on the freedom of the press," but the government took no further action against the perpetrators.

In January police arrested four suspects on homicide charges for their alleged involvement in the October 2012 attack on Popular Radio in Yacuiba, Tarija Department. During the attack broadcaster Fernando Vidal and studio technician Karen Arce suffered severe burns. Minister of Communication Amanda Davila denounced the attack, and Government Minister Carlos Romero pledged a rapid and thorough investigation. On June 5, one of the suspects, Antonio Camacho, was released on parole, but he fled, and his whereabouts were unknown at year's end. The other three suspects remained in preventive detention awaiting trial at year's end.

Internet Freedom

There were no government restrictions on access to the internet or credible reports that the government monitored e-mail or internet chat rooms without appropriate legal authority, but Vice President Garcia Linera stated in October 2012 that the government recorded the names of people who insulted President Morales on social media sites.

The 2012 census found that 9 percent of households had internet access, but families in rural regions of the country reported more limited at-home access. For instance, the census found that only 3 percent of households in Potosi Department maintained internet access in their residences. An August 2012 Captura Consulting study found that 53 percent of citizens occasionally used the internet but that fewer than 15 percent used it on a daily basis.

Academic Freedom and Cultural Events

There were no government restrictions on academic freedom or cultural events.

b. Freedom of Peaceful Assembly and Association

The constitution provides for freedom of assembly and association, and the government generally respected these rights. The law requires a permit for most demonstrations, but the government rarely enforced the provisions, and most protesters demonstrated without obtaining permits.

Freedom of Assembly

While most demonstrations were peaceful, occasionally demonstrators carried weapons, including clubs, machetes, firearms, and dynamite. Security forces (police and on occasion the military) at times dispersed protest groups carrying weapons or threatening government and private facilities.

On February 14, police used tear gas to prevent a group of peaceful protesters from entering the central government square to demand the government pass a law to prevent gender-based violence. Authorities granted the protesters access to the square after several female cabinet ministers participating in the march intervened.

At year's end authorities continued to investigate the 2011 case in which police forces in Yucumo, Beni, used tear gas and other methods to disband a peaceful march by indigenous leaders protesting the construction of a highway through their land. In January 2012, the prosecutor ruled out the involvement of President Morales, Vice President Garcia Linera, and former minister of government and current ambassador to the UN Sacha Llorenti. On August 1, however, former ministry of government lawyer Boris Villegas, detained on charges of extortion related to the Jacob Ostreicher case, told prosecutors that Llorenti ordered police to intervene in the march (see sections 1.d. and 4.). On September 10, prosecutors sent eight questions to President Morales to provide information about his involvement in the case, and on September 30, Morales responded in writing that he did not order nor did he know who approved the police intervention. Former police commander Oscar Munoz, detained in 2011 on charges related to police aggression, remained under house arrest, and prosecutors did not present charges against additional suspects by the year's end.

Freedom of Association

The constitution provides for freedom of association, and the government generally respected these rights.

c. Freedom of Religion

See the Department of State's *International Religious Freedom Report* at www.state.gov/j/drl/irf/rpt.

d. Freedom of Movement, Internally Displaced Persons, Protection of Refugees, and Stateless Persons

The constitution and law provide for freedom of internal movement, foreign travel, emigration, and repatriation. The law prohibits travel 24 hours before elections and on census days and restricts foreign and domestic travel for up to three months as a penalty for persons who do not vote.

The government cooperated with the Office of the UN High Commissioner for Refugees (UNHCR) and other humanitarian organizations in providing protection and assistance to refugees, returning refugees, asylum seekers, stateless persons, and other persons of concern.

Exile: The UNHCR reported that as of January 2013 there were 618 Bolivian refugees living in exile abroad and 156 Bolivians in the process of seeking asylum.

National Convergence Party Senator Roger Pinto, who was granted political asylum by the Brazilian government in June 2012, fled to Brazil on August 23. Pinto had been living in the Brazilian embassy since May 2012, after the Bolivian government refused to grant safe passage, accusing him of 21 criminal charges and convicting him on one corruption count in June. Pinto remained in Brazil at year's end.

On August 8, Tarija District Attorney Gilbert Munoz brought a new corruption charge against suspended Tarija governor Mario Cossio, on which grounds Judge Carsen Romero de Pena ordered Cossio's arrest. Minister of Transparency Nardi Suxo stated in June that Cossio faced 22 other criminal charges. Cossio was suspended from his position in 2010 on corruption charges, and in 2011 he was granted asylum in Paraguay, where he remained at year's end.

Protection of Refugees

The UNHCR reported that 733 refugees from more than 20 countries resided in the country. According to media reports, most refugees were Peruvian and lived in La Paz, Cochabamba, and Santa Cruz. The state did not provide temporary protection or resettlement services to these persons.

Access to Asylum: The law provides for the granting of asylum or refugee status, and the government has established a system for providing protection to refugees through the National Commission on Refugees.

Refoulement: On March 19 and 20, the Inter-American Court for Human Rights (IA Court) heard arguments in the case of the *Family Pacheco Tineo v. Bolivia*. The family alleged that in 2001 the government violated their refugee status by forcibly returning them to Peru, where they were imprisoned. The family submitted a petition to the IACHR in 2002, which found in 2004 that the government had violated several provisions of the American Convention on Human Rights. The IACHR referred the case to the IA Court in February2012, but the court had not issued a ruling at year's end.

Section 3. Respect for Political Rights: The Right of Citizens to Change Their Government

The constitution and law provide citizens the right to change their government peacefully, and citizens exercised this right through periodic, free, and fair elections based on universal suffrage. Many citizens of voting age, particularly in rural areas, lacked the identity documents necessary to vote. A broad spectrum of political parties and citizens' groups functioned openly. Elections for national offices and municipal governments are scheduled every five years.

Elections and Political Participation

Recent Elections: Monitoring groups from the Organization of American States (OAS), the European Union, and the Carter Center considered the 2009 national presidential and legislative elections peaceful, free, and fair.

The nation's first judicial elections, held in October 2011, were deemed free and fair by observers from the OAS and the Union of South American States. Electoral laws, however, prohibited media access to the candidates prior to the elections, and opposition leaders claimed the pre-selection of candidates by congress rendered the vote "legal but not legitimate."

Political Parties: There are no undue restrictions on political parties, but some opposition political leaders alleged the government's charges against some elected officials and opposition political leaders were politically motivated. On May 3, Margoth Arriaga, mayor of San Ramon in Beni Department and member of the Beni First Party, was arrested and placed in preventive detention on corruption charges. On May 6, she suffered a stress-induced heart attack and was taken to the German Busch Hospital in Trinidad for treatment. At least five court hearings in her case were canceled without explanation, and at year's end she remained in preventive detention without formal charges or a sentence.

Beni Governor Ernesto Suarez (PODEMOS Party), who resigned to allow for a special election on January 20, remained under investigation at year's end. In 2011 Suarez was suspended from office on corruption charges. On July 2, former ministry of government lawyer Boris Villenas, held on charges of extortion related to the Jacob Ostreicher case, told prosecutors that former minister of government Sacha Llorenti built a false case against Suarez in order to remove him from office (see sections 1.d. and 4). On July 10, Suarez filed a lawsuit alleging sedition against Presidency Minister Juan Ramon Quintana, Llorenti, and Supreme Court President Gonzalo Hurtado.

On February 5, the Constitutional Court announced its decision striking down four articles of the Department Autonomy Law that allowed the government to suspend from office elected officials who were under investigation but who had not been sentenced. The Constitutional Court decision was not automatically applied retroactively, and suspended officials had to file legal appeals to resume their elected functions. At least one official was reinstated. On February 7, the Potosi City Council restored Social Alliance Party member Rene Joaquino Cabrera to his position as mayor. He was suspended from office in 2010 after being charged but not convicted of corruption. Suspended governors Ernesto Suarez and Mario Cossio and approximately 20 other officials were removed from office under the unconstitutional provisions (see sections 1.d.).

Participation of Women and Minorities: The law mandates gender parity in the candidate selection process at all levels of government. The gender parity laws increased female representation. Women made up 44 percent of the Senate, 23 percent of the lower chamber of congress, 28 percent of department legislative assemblies, and 43 percent of town councils. Women held seven of the 20 cabinet positions. Women also accounted for 33 percent of the Supreme Court, 57 percent of the Constitutional Court, and 43 percent of the National Land and Dispute Court. Women remained significantly underrepresented in municipal executive positions; for example, only 7 percent of mayors were female. On May 20, Gina Reque Teran became the first woman to achieve the rank of general in the armed forces.

Credible NGOs reported that women participating in politics sometimes faced violence and harassment. In some cases winning female candidates reported they were threatened with violence in order to force their resignation so a male alternative candidate could assume the position. The Association of Female Mayors and Alderwomen stated that between 2000 and 2009, its members reported 249 cases of politically motivated harassment and violence. On February 6, community members burned down the house of Cuatro Canadas mayor Dominga Fernandez in an attempt to force her resignation. On August 27, Petronila Aliaga, elected to the Colquencha town council in La Paz Department, resigned from office, stating she feared the constant threats and verbal attacks she suffered from some male community leaders.

The constitution and electoral law set aside seven special indigenous districts to increase the participation of minority indigenous communities in the lower house of congress. One of these seven seats is reserved for an Afro-Bolivian representative. The law also required the pre-selection of an undefined number of indigenous candidates for the 2011 judicial elections. Indigenous persons held 40 percent of the positions on the four highest courts.

Section 4. Corruption and Lack of Transparency in Government

The law provides criminal penalties for corruption by officials, but the government did not implement the law effectively, and officials often engaged in corrupt practices with impunity. There were numerous reports of government corruption.

Corruption: According to the World Bank's 2011 worldwide governance indicators, government corruption and lack of transparency remained serious problems. According to Transparency International's 2013 *Global Corruption Barometer*, 86 percent of citizens believed the police were corrupt or extremely corrupt, and 76 percent labeled the country's judiciary as corrupt or extremely corrupt.

Police corruption remained a significant problem, partially due to low salaries and lack of training. On August 31, U.S. authorities arrested police officer Fabricio Ormachea Aliga in Miami on charges of extortion. Ormachea, an investigator in the police anticorruption unit, allegedly promised to suspend a pending investigation involving a Bolivian living in Miami in exchange for approximately 205,000 bolivianos ($30,000).

There was also widespread corruption in the country's judiciary. In February Attorney General Ramiro Guerrero stated that nearly 100 prosecutors were under investigation for corruption and other charges or had already been convicted and suspended. President of the Council of Judges Cristina Mamani stated that in the first six months of the year, there were 1,698 lawsuits filed against judges, jurists, and prosecutors. Of the 1,698 suits, 428 resulted in penalties, 300 were dismissed, and the remaining cases were pending. The majority of guilty cases resulted in warnings and minor administrative penalties, and only three judges were dismissed from their positions.

There was little progress in the investigation of 14 government officials, including Fernando Rivera Tardio, Denis Efrain Rodas Limachi, Boris Villegas, and Jose Manuel Antezana Pinaya, who were arrested in November and December 2012 in connection with the Jacob Ostreicher case. Former Ministry of Government official Villegas made several public allegations about the extortion network's involvement in several other open cases, including the corruption case against former Beni governor Ernesto Suarez. The Ministry of Government's Transparency Unit announced that as of May 28, lawsuits had been opened against the extortion network for alleged abuse in at least 24 pending cases, but at year's end all of the suspects remained in preventive detention without trial (see section 1.d.).

The Ministry of Anticorruption and Transparency and the Prosecutor's Office are responsible for combating corruption, but most corrupt officials operated with impunity. On August 15, Transparency Minister Nardy Suxo reported that of the

400 cases she referred to the Attorney General's Office, only 80 resulted in convictions. Cases involving allegations of corruption against the president and vice president require congressional approval before prosecutors may initiate legal proceedings.

Whistleblower Protection: The law provides protection to public and private employees for making internal disclosures and lawful public disclosures of evidence of corruption. The transparency minister is responsible for protecting the identity of whistleblowers.

Financial Disclosure: The law requires public officials to report potential personal and financial conflicts of interest and to declare their income and assets. The law mandates that elected and appointed officials disclose their financial information to the auditor general, but their declarations are not available to the public. According to the law, noncompliance shall result in internal sanctions, including dismissal. The auditor general must refer cases involving criminal activity to the Attorney General's office.

Public Access to Information: No laws provide for access to government information.

Section 5. Governmental Attitude Regarding International and Nongovernmental Investigation of Alleged Violations of Human Rights

A number of domestic and international human rights groups generally operated without government restriction, investigating and publishing their findings on human rights cases. NGOs and the human rights ombudsman complained that senior government officials and government security forces sometimes refused to cooperate with their investigations.

Commander of the Armed Forces General Edwin de la Fuente refused to respond to Human Rights Ombudsman Rolando Villena's requests throughout the year for information about the unexplained deaths of at least six military personnel (see section 1.a). Senior government officials also sometimes sought to undermine the credibility of the human rights ombudsman. After the ombudsman recommended on September 25 that the government temporally recall Ambassador Sacha Llorenti to meet with prosecutors about his involvement in the 2011 violent police action against indigenous protesters in Yucumo, Beni, President Morales accused the ombudsman of being "an instrument of the right" (see section 2.b.).

Government Human Rights Bodies: The constitution establishes a human rights ombudsman with a six-year term. Confirmation to the position of ombudsman requires a two-thirds majority vote of approval from both houses of the National Assembly. The ombudsman is charged with overseeing the defense and promotion of human rights, specifically defending citizens against government abuses. The constitution also affords the ombudsman the right to propose new legislation and to recommend modifications to existing laws and government policies. There are also ombudsmen to oversee each of the country's nine departments. They report directly to the national ombudsman. The ombudsman's office operated with adequate resources from the government and foreign NGOs, allowing the institution to operate effectively. On June 16, Ombudsman Rolando Villena Villegas requested that the government increase its budgetary contribution to the institution, noting that in 2013, 40 percent of funding came from the government and the remaining 60 percent from international organizations.

Both houses of congress have Human Rights Committees, which propose laws and policies to promote and protect human rights. Congressional deputies and senators sit on the committees for one-year terms.

Section 6. Discrimination, Societal Abuses, and Trafficking in Persons

The constitution prohibits discrimination based on race, gender, disability, language, sexual orientation, gender identity, or social status, but the government did not effectively enforce the law to protect all populations.

Women

Rape and Domestic Violence: Rape and domestic violence remained serious and underreported problems. On March 9, President Morales signed the Comprehensive Law to Guarantee Women a Life Free from Violence, which increases penalties for rape of an adult from four to 10 years' imprisonment to 15- to 20-year terms. The new law also strengthens penalties for physical and psychological abuse. Domestic abuse that results in injury is punishable by three- to six-years' imprisonment, and the penalty for serious physical or psychological harm is a five- to 12-year sentence. The law also criminalizes forced abortion, defined as any violence that fatally interrupts a pregnancy, with a four- to eight-year sentence. Although the new law enhances the role of the police to prevent and punish domestic violence offenders by creating the Special Force in the Fight against Domestic Violence, conviction rates were low. Women's rights organizations reported the new police units did not have sufficient resources and that frontline officers lacked proper training about their new investigatory authorities under the law. Women's organizations also reported that the law's stringent new penalties discouraged some women from reporting domestic abuse by their spouses on whom they were economically dependent.

Sexual violence and rape continued to be serious and widespread problems. A study by the NGO the Women's Coordinator found that of the sexual violence cases reported through the legal system, 58 percent involved the rape of an adult and 10 percent the rape of a minor. The Center for Sexual Education and Research reported rapists accounted for the second-largest number of 1,700 inmates surveyed, although most rapists were never sentenced. There also were cases of sexual violence that resulted in deaths. The Center for the Women's Information and Development (CIDEM) reported that from January through June, 81 women were killed in incidents of domestic violence. In 12 of the cases, perpetrators committed rape before killing the victim.

Domestic violence remained a serious problem. According to CIDEM, 70 percent of women suffered physical, sexual, or psychological abuse during their lifetime. According to a CIDEM and Emancipation Fund study, the number of reported domestic violence cases increased by 37 percent between 2007 and 2011, the most recent data available, reaching an annual total of 109,062 in 2011. Rape and domestic violence cases were underreported, due to lack of confidence in authority systems, fear of further violence and retribution, and social stigma. The study also found that only 9 percent of the cases over the five-year period had been legally resolved and less than 0.5 percent of the cases resulted in a prison sentence for the accused. The Women's Coordinator study found that 91 percent of domestic violence victims were women and girls.

Sexual Harassment: The law considers sexual harassment a civil offense. There were no reports on the extent of sexual harassment, but observers generally acknowledged it was widespread.

Reproductive Rights: The government recognizes the right of couples and individuals to decide freely and responsibly the number, spacing, and timing of their children. Health clinics and local health NGOs operated freely in disseminating information on family planning under the guidance of the Ministry of Health and Sports. According to the joint World Health Organization (WHO), UN, and World Bank's *Trends in Maternal Mortality* study for 1990 to 2010, the maternal mortality rate was estimated to be 190 per 100,000 live births in 2008. Major factors influencing the high maternal mortality rate included poor sanitation and lack of access to proper health facilities. According to WHO, nearly 85 percent of women received prenatal care, 28 percent received postnatal care, and skilled attendants assisted 66 percent of births.

Poverty, discrimination, and lack of access to sexual education led to low rates of contraceptive use. Ramiro Claure, director of the family planning organization Marie Stopes International Bolivia, reported that 81 percent of women did not use modern forms of birth control, and an Emancipation Fund study found that nearly 40 percent of women did not use any type of birth control method. The Population Reference Bureau reported that 34 percent of married women used modern contraceptives. Access to birth control and education about reproductive rights was more limited in rural areas, where the fertility rate was nearly twice as high as in urban areas. On September 17, the Ministry of Health formed an inter-institutional committee, including the UN Population Fund and the Pan American Health Organization, to launch new programs aimed at increasing use of contraceptives.

Discrimination: Women are entitled to the same legal rights as men but generally did not enjoy a social status equal to that of men. Traditional prejudices and social conditions remained obstacles to advancement. The minimum-wage law treats men and women equally; however, women generally earned less than men for equal work. In January the National Statistics Institute reported that the average salary for women was approximately half the average salary for men and that the wage disparity was greater in urban areas than in rural communities. Women sometimes complained that employers were reluctant to hire them due to the additional costs, such as expenses related to maternity leave, in a woman's benefits package. The gender gap in hiring appeared widest for positions requiring higher education. Most women in urban areas worked in the informal economy and the services and trade sectors, including domestic service and micro-business, whereas in rural areas the majority of economically active women worked in agriculture. Some young girls left school early to work at home or in the informal economy. The 2012 census showed that the overall literacy gap between men and women fell to 4.9 percent from 12.4 percent in 2001 and that the literacy gap was virtually nonexistent among individuals between the ages of 15 and 25.

The rate of female participation in government was high, but there were reports that female policymakers faced discrimination, violence, and harassment.

The Ministry of Justice's Office of Equal Opportunities is responsible for developing and implementing public policies to eliminate discrimination against women.

Children

Birth Registration: Citizenship is derived both through birth within the country's territory (unless on diplomatic status) and from one's parent(s). Birth certificates are registered either by a notary's affirmation of the certificate or through testimony of two adults regarding a child's parentage. Registered birth certificates are necessary to obtain national identification cards. The Civil Registry reported that 56 percent of Bolivians were registered within one year of their birth and 97 percent by the age of 12. Civil Registry Director Jose Pardo stated that approximately 10 percent of the population, or one million individuals, did not have birth certificates.

Child Abuse: Domestic violence against children and school bullying continued at high rates. The human rights ombudsman stated seven in 10 children suffered physical or psychological mistreatment in their homes, schools, or places of work. Education Minister Roberto Aguilar estimated 10 percent of children were victims of sexual aggression. A 2011 CIDEM study, the most recent available, reported there were 7,466 reported cases of psychological abuse and 2,733 reported cases of physical abuse against children. Only 684 cases were referred to the legal system, including 373 cases of rape and five killings.

The Comprehensive Law to Guarantee Women a Life Free from Violence, approved March 9, strengthens penalties for rape of a child under the age of 14 to 20- to 25-years' imprisonment. The penalty for consensual sex with an adolescent 14 to 18 years old is two to six years' imprisonment. The human rights ombudsman stated that his office received reports of approximately 14,000 child rape cases annually.

Government authorities took action to reduce violence and harassment in public schools, but abuse remained a significant problem. On January 2, the minister of education released Resolution 001, which mandates that school administrators implement policies to prevent violence and discrimination in public schools. In April, the human rights ombudsman reported six in 10 students had suffered some form of verbal or physical assault at school, and the minister of education announced that as of July 30, authorities had identified 60 cases of child abuse and harassment in public schools and that several teachers were under investigation for sexual abuse, including rape.

Forced and Early Marriage: According to the Population Reference Bureau, 22 percent of women ages 20 to 24 were married by age 18. The minimum age for marriage is 14 for girls and 16 for boys. Marriages between adolescents under 18 must be approved by the minors' parents or guardians. The UN Population Fund reported the prevalence of forced and early marriage was on the decline in both urban and rural areas of four of the country's nine departments--La Paz, Pando, Chuquisaca, and Beni.

Sexual Exploitation of Children: Commercial sexual exploitation of children is punishable with 15- to 20-year prison sentences, but it remained a serious problem. The law also prohibits child pornography, punishable with 10- to 15- year sentences.

Displaced Children: According to the human rights ombudsman, 6,000 children lived on the streets of major cities.

Institutionalized Children: Child advocacy organizations reported that many government-run shelters housed both child-abuse victims and juvenile delinquents. There were also reports of abuse and negligence in some shelters. The La Paz Department Social Work Service Director Cristina Rojas reported that of the region's 380 shelters, including centers for abuse victims, orphans, and school students, only 30 had received government accreditation for meeting minimal standards. On April 16, authorities removed two minors from the Casa Esperanza shelter in Achocalla, La Paz Department, after they were allegedly abused and kept in unhygienic conditions.

International Child Abductions: The country is not a party to the 1980 Hague Convention on the Civil Aspects of International Child Abduction. For country-specific information see the Department of State's report at http://travel.state.gov/abduction/country/country_5976.html.

Anti-Semitism

The Jewish population numbered fewer than 1,000. Jewish community leaders stated that there were no reports of anti-Semitic acts.

Trafficking in Persons

See the Department of State's *Trafficking in Persons Report* at www.state.gov/j/tip.

Persons with Disabilities

The law prohibits discrimination against persons with physical, sensory, intellectual, and mental disabilities in employment, education, air travel and other transportation, access to health care, or the provision of other state services. The law requires access for wheelchair users to all public and private buildings, duty-free import of orthopedic devices, and a 50 percent reduction in public transportation fares for persons with disabilities. The constitution and law also require communication outlets and government agencies to offer services and publications in sign language and Braille, but the government did not effectively enforce these provisions. In addition, societal discrimination kept many persons with disabilities at home from an early age, limiting their integration into society and restricting their right to participate in civic affairs. The Research Center for Socioeconomic Development reported that only an estimated 13,000 children with disabilities, or 6 percent of the population of youth with disabilities, had regular access to education. There was no information available regarding patterns of abuse in educational and mental health facilities.

The National Committee for Persons with Disabilities is responsible for protecting the rights of persons with disabilities.

The government provides an annual pension of 1,000 bolivianos ($146) to persons with "serious or very serious" conditions. In July 2012 the Ministry of Health launched the National Registry for People with Disabilities. The registry included 40,368 people, of whom 36 percent reported physical disabilities, 30 percent mental disabilities, and 20 percent multiple disabilities.

National/Racial/Ethnic Minorities

Afro-Bolivian community leaders reported that employment discrimination remained common and that public officials, particularly the police, discriminated in the provision of services. Afro-Bolivians also reported the widespread use of discriminatory language.

Indigenous People

In the 2012 census, approximately 41 percent of the population over the age of 15 self-identified as indigenous, primarily from the Quechua and Aymara communities. The IACHR reported that 70 percent of indigenous persons lived in poverty or extreme poverty with little access to education or minimal services to support human health, such as clean drinking water and sanitation systems. The government carried out programs to increase access to potable water and sanitation in rural areas where indigenous people predominated. The government's Indigenous Fund initiated support in 2010 for development projects designed primarily to benefit indigenous communities, but the media reported in September that the fund had accumulated 1.37 billion bolivianos ($200 million) in unallocated funding.

Indigenous lands were not fully demarcated, and land reform remained a central political issue. Historically, some indigenous persons shared lands collectively under the "ayllu" system, which was not legally recognized during the transition to private property laws. Despite laws mandating reallocation and titling of lands, recognition and demarcation of indigenous lands were not completed.

Authorities continued their investigation into the forceful dispersing by police of a peaceful march in 2011 by indigenous leaders protesting the construction of a highway through their land. At year's end the government had taken limited investigatory action, and no suspects were arrested (see section 2.b.).

Indigenous communities were well represented in government and politics, but they bore a disproportionate share of poverty and unemployment. Government educational and health services remained unavailable to many indigenous groups living in remote areas.

Societal Abuses, Discrimination, and Acts of Violence Based on Sexual Orientation and Gender Identity

The constitution prohibits discrimination based on sexual orientation and gender identity, and citizens are allowed to change their name and gender on their official identification cards. Nonetheless, societal discrimination against LGBT persons was common, and government action to counter it was limited.

The director general of the Fight Against Racism and All Forms of Discrimination announced that anti-LGBT discrimination was the most common form of discrimination reported during the first quarter of the year. Credible LGBT organizations reported police violence against and unwillingness to aid LGBT persons. An Emancipation Fund study found that 86 percent of surveyed LGBT individuals reported suffering physical or verbal abuse by police officers. The study also noted that of those surveyed, 85 percent reported discrimination in educational institutions, 78 percent in health facilities, and 65 percent at work; in addition, nearly half reported discrimination by family members.

The transgender community remained particularly vulnerable to abuse and violence. On May 10, three transgender women were physically assaulted in Cochabamba. Authorities arrested four suspects. One suspect was placed in preventive detention on discrimination and assault charges, but he was not sentenced by year's end. Authorities did not report any progress in the investigation of the October 2012 killing of Luisa Duran, a self-identified transgender woman, whose death LGBT organizations alleged was hate motivated.

Other Societal Violence or Discrimination

Although the law prohibits discrimination against persons with HIV/AIDS, pervasive discrimination persisted and, in at least one case, resulted in a killing. Ministry of Health authorities reported that discrimination against persons with HIV/AIDS was most severe in indigenous communities, where the government was least successful in diagnosing cases. In August 2012 the Ministry of Health reported that of the people with HIV/AIDS surveyed, 32 percent had suffered insults or verbal abuse, 20 percent had been threatened, and 22 percent had been victims of violent aggression. The study also noted that 20 percent of those surveyed reported discrimination in government service provision at hospitals and schools and that many persons with HIV/AIDS did not report acts of discrimination due to fear. On July 23, Police Coronel Ramiro Magne reported that the police found the body of an HIV-positive man in El Alto. Magne stated the victim was killed and his corpse burned after he publicly revealed his medical condition. At year's end authorities had not arrested any suspects in connection with the killing.

Vigilante justice remained a serious problem, especially in rural communities and in El Alto. The media reported that between 2008 and June 2012, 54 persons were killed in acts of mob violence. In many cases the victims were killed for alleged crimes. For example, on May 28, community members in El Alto's District 14 Bautista Saavedra neighborhood, La Paz Department, burned a man alive after he was accused of trying to extort a local business owner.

Section 7. Worker Rights

a. Freedom of Association and the Right to Collective Bargaining

The law, including related regulations and statutory instruments, provides for the freedom of association, the right to strike, and the right to organize and bargain collectively, and it prohibits antiunion discrimination. The constitution allows any working individual to join a union and provides for the right to strike. The law does not require government approval for strikes and allows peaceful strikers to occupy business or government offices.

Workers may form a union in any private company of 20 or more employees, but the law requires that at least 50 percent of the workforce be in favor. The law requires prior government authorization to establish a union and confirm its elected leadership, permits only one union per enterprise, and allows the government to dissolve unions by administrative fiat. The law also requires that members of union executive boards be Bolivian by birth. The labor code prohibits some public employees from forming unions but permits government employees in the education, health-care, and transportation sectors to organize.

The government enforced applicable laws, but it was slow to do so and continued to use an outdated labor code instead of the constitution. The National Labor Court handles complaints of antiunion discrimination, but rulings took a year or more. The court ruled in favor of discharged workers in some cases and required their reinstatement. Union leaders stated that problems often had been resolved or were no longer relevant by the time the court ruled. Government remedies and penalties were often ineffective for this reason. There was at least one decision in an antiunion discrimination case during the year. The company was fined 16,000 bolivianos ($2,330) for allegedly retaliating against two employees who were trying to form a union.

Freedom of association was limited by the government and under resourced labor courts. Moreover, the minimum requirement of 20 workers proved an onerous restriction, as an estimated 72 percent of enterprises had fewer than 20 employees. Labor inspectors may attend union meetings and monitor union activities.

Some public-sector workers (including teachers, transportation workers, and health-care workers) were legally unionized and actively participated as members of the Bolivian Workers' Union without penalty. General and solidarity strikes are protected by the constitution. Collective bargaining and voluntary direct negotiations between employers and workers without government participation was limited. Most collective bargaining agreements were restricted to addressing wages.

Violence during labor demonstrations continued to be a serious problem. During a labor strike organized by the Bolivian Labor Central union, at least 30 individuals, including both protesters and police officers, were injured between May 5 and 15. On May 6, near Parotani, Cochabamba Department, two protesters were allegedly shot and wounded. Also on May 6, three police officers were allegedly detained for two days and physically abused by protesters near Huanuni, in Oruro Department. Despite President Morales' 2012 executive order outlawing the use of dynamite during public protests, the practice remained common. On May 8, protesters near Caihuasi, Oruro Department, badly damaged a public bridge with dynamite. Authorities did not report progress in the investigation of the September 2012 death of Hector Choque, who died after a stick of dynamite exploded in his vicinity during a protest.

b. Prohibition of Forced or Compulsory Labor

The law prohibits all forms of forced or compulsory labor. The law penalizes labor exploitation, forced labor, and other forms of servitude with 10- to 15-years' imprisonment for exploitation of adults and 15- to 20-years' imprisonment for exploitation of children.

In some cases the government did not effectively enforce the law banning forced labor. Ministry of Labor officials noted that lack of resources prevented more thorough enforcement of the law.

There were reports of forced child labor (see section 7.c.). Members of indigenous communities continued to be vulnerable to forced labor, including in domestic service and the agriculture sector. For instance, a report released by an NGO in 2012 noted that workers involved in the production of Brazil nuts from the Amazon region and Chaco regions may be vulnerable to forced labor, highlighting indicators of forced labor such as induced indebtedness, withholding and nonpayment of wages, and retention of identity documents. The report stressed the government actively combated forced labor but had a limited capacity, especially in isolated areas.

Also see the Department of State's *Trafficking in Persons Report* at www.state.gov/j/tip.

c. Prohibition of Child Labor and Minimum Age for Employment

The law prohibits all paid work by children under the age of 14 as well as a range of dangerous, immoral, and unhealthy types of work for minors under 18. Labor law permits apprenticeship for 12- to 14-year-old children with various formal but poorly enforced restrictions that the International Labor Organization (ILO) criticized. Children under 14 worked in a variety of industries, including dangerous sectors such as mining and agriculture.

The Ministry of Labor is responsible for enforcing child labor laws, including laws pertaining to the minimum age and maximum hours for child workers, school completion requirements, and health and safety conditions for children in the workplace; however, authorities did not effectively enforce the laws. Resources were not sufficient to prevent child labor. Information was not provided on the penalties for violation of child labor laws and the effectiveness of such penalties. There were five Ministry of Labor inspectors dedicated to detecting child labor, and during the year they conducted approximately 50 inspections. Government authorities could not verify the number of minors removed from such labor.

The Bolivian Institute for International Trade, with support from the government, worked with the sugar association to eliminate child labor throughout the sugar production chain. The institute created a triple seal to certify that companies were free of child labor, forced labor, and discrimination. Up to 500 sugar manufacturers continued to participate in the program, but none had received the triple seal by year's end.

Child labor remained a serious problem. The Bolivian National Statistics Institute estimated in 2013 that 381,000 Bolivian children were engaged in labor activities, but according to a 2008 ILO report, 849,000 children, approximately 28 percent of children between the ages of five and 17, worked at least one hour a week. Of the working children, 397,000 worked in urban areas and 452,000 in rural communities. Approximately 491,000 of the working children were between the ages of five and 13, of whom 89 percent worked in dangerous sectors or conditions.

Urban children sold goods, shined shoes, and assisted transport operators. Rural children often worked with parents from an early age, generally in agriculture. A report released by an NGO in September, based on 2010-11 data, reported instances of child labor in the production of corn and Brazil nuts. The report noted that families typically carried out Brazil nut-harvesting and that child labor existed.

Researchers also found that some children worked in Brazil nut-processing factories, including at night. Children also worked as domestic servants. There were reports that children were victims of forced labor in mining, agriculture, and as domestic servants.

Also see the Department of Labor's *Findings on the Worst Forms of Child Labor* at www.dol.gov/ilab/programs/ocft/tda.htm.

d. Acceptable Conditions of Work

The government raised the minimum monthly wage by 22.6 percent, to 1,000 bolivianos ($146) for the public and private sectors. The government's official estimate of the poverty income level was 495 bolivianos ($72) per month. Labor laws establish a maximum workweek of 48 hours and limit the workday to eight hours for men. The laws also set a 40-hour workweek for women, prohibit women from working at night, mandate rest periods, and require premium pay for work above a standard workweek. The law stipulates a minimum of 15 days' annual leave. The Ministry of Labor sets occupational health and safety standards and monitors compliance. The law mandates that the standards apply uniformly to all industries and sectors.

The government did not effectively enforce these laws. The Ministry of Labor's Bureau of Occupational Safety has responsibility for the protection of workers' health and safety, but the relevant standards were poorly enforced. There were 78 inspectors in the entire country. The law provides for penalties for noncompliance, but enforcement was not effective, and the fines of 1,000 to 10,000 bolivianos ($146-1,460) were insufficient to deter violations. An estimated two-thirds of workers were part of the informal economy. There was no significant government effort to formalize or enforce labor laws in this portion of the economy.

A national tripartite committee of business, labor, and government representatives is responsible for monitoring and improving occupational safety and health standards and enforcement. The Ministry of Labor maintained offices for worker inquiries, complaints, and reports of unfair labor practices and unsafe working conditions, but it was unclear whether the offices were effective in regulating working conditions. While the government did not keep official statistics, there were reports that workers died due to unsafe conditions, particularly in the mining and construction sectors. There were no significant government efforts to improve safety conditions. Working conditions in cooperative-operated mines remained poor. Miners worked with no scheduled rest for long periods in dangerous, unhealthy conditions.

The Construction Workers Union Confederation reported that as of August 18, 11 construction workers suffered fatal work-related injuries, four more than in 2012. The union also reported that of the 1,350 nationally registered construction companies, at least 60 percent reported some form of accident, resulting in injury to an employee.